Conflict Resolution
Activities That Work!

by Kathleen M. Hollenbeck

SCHOLASTIC
PROFESSIONAL BOOKS

New York • Toronto • London • Auckland • Sydney
Mexico City • New Delhi • Hong Kong

Dedication

This book is dedicated to those who spend their lives teaching and exercising the art of peaceful communication. In all walks of life, it is a priceless gift.

Acknowledgments

Special thanks to Linda Harris for her dedicated consultation on this book. Linda Harris is a staff developer and training consultant for the Resolving Conflict Creatively Program, Educators for Social Responsibility Metro, Creative Response to Conflict, the Learning Institute for Educators, and the NYC Board of Education's Professional Development Program. She coordinates a conflict resolution/peer mediation program at PS 230 in Brooklyn and teaches at Bank Street College of Education.

Cover design by Norma Ortiz

Cover illustration by Cynthia Fisher

Interior illustrations by James Graham Hale

Interior design by Sydney Wright

ISBN: 0-439-11113-7

Copyright © 2001 by Kathleen M. Hollenbeck

Contents

* = activities with a reproducible page for students

Introduction

Conflict, in all of its forms, pervades our lives in ways both good and bad. Sometimes conflict effects positive change. Faced with friction, people can learn to respect differences of opinion and allow others to be themselves. They can learn to share, work together, and coexist in a world in which individualism and diversity are both embraced and rejected. At other times, conflict spirals into negativity, leading to violence and abuse and threatening safety, security, and peace.

Handled correctly, most conflicts can be resolved to the satisfaction of everyone involved. Children have within their grasp the tools needed for resolving conflicts peacefully, yet most have little idea how to use them. That's what conflict resolution is all about: training people to respond effectively to conflict and preventing the harm that results from emotions that have spun out of control. Conflict resolution is not a quick fix or a bandage applied in the wake of a problem. It is a process of learning, a means of preventing discord and hostility by teaching children and adults to react in ways that promote peace, respect, understanding, and communication.

Conflict Resolution Activities That Work! is packed with quick, easy-to-use activities and techniques designed to help second and third graders learn to speak, act, and react with understanding, self-control, and respect for themselves and for others. As you share these, your students will learn to identify their feelings and to recognize characteristics of anger in its beginning and advanced stages. They'll find out what to do when anger builds, how to calm themselves and others down, and how to resolve a conflict so that everyone benefits. With conflict resolution in practice, everyone can win.

How to Use This Book

As a teacher, you are in a prime position to affect the ways in which your students view and handle conflict. You are not responsible for their responses, yet your influence can last a lifetime. In this book, you'll find thoughtful activities that teach students effective conflict prevention and resolution strategies. You might already be employing some of these techniques in your classroom; others may be less familiar. As you review and share these strategies with students, you will empower them with peacemaking skills.

In *Teaching Conflict Resolution Through Children's Literature* (Scholastic, 1994) William J. Kreidler describes "the Peaceable Classroom Model." This approach views the classroom as a "caring and respectful community" and focuses on five themes: cooperating, communicating, expressing emotions, appreciating diversity, and resolving conflict. *Conflict Resolution Activities That Work!* includes activities that promote each of these key themes. For more on the Peaceable Classroom Model, refer to William J. Kreidler's books, *Creative Conflict Resolution* (Scott Foresman and Co., 1984) and *Elementary Perspectives: Teaching Concepts of Peace and Conflict* (Educators for Social Responsibility, 1991).

Conflict Resolution Activities That Work! is designed for second and third graders, but the skills it reinforces are appropriate for all ages. These activities can be used anytime, and they fit easily into any core curriculum. Most activities require no advance planning, other than duplicating a reproducible or two. The techniques and activities are intended to heighten student awareness of effective ways to prevent and resolve conflict so they will be better equipped to handle real-life situations.

No prerequisite training is required to use this book. Those who have never studied conflict resolution will find the background information they need within these pages as well as dozens of reinforcing activities. Those who have attended workshops on conflict resolution, social decision-making, and related topics will find this book helpful in applying what they've learned to the classroom in fun and meaningful ways.

Although the activities in this book can be used in any order, I recommend that you begin with section one, entitled Feelings First. Emotions are powerful triggers for conflict; helping students identify emotions and realize their effects can provide a solid foundation for preventing and resolving conflict. As you explore and share these topics, you may find the resources listed on page 64 helpful.

The best way to reinforce conflict resolution skills is to practice. The activities in this book build students' confidence in their ability to solve and prevent problems. Some, such as the student play, are intended for one-time use. Others, such as puppet plays, story strips, and conflict cubes, can be used over and over again. Place story starters in a learning center for use all year long, or incorporate them into an interactive bulletin board display. Explore conflict with the picture books examined in the third section (pages 44–52); then apply the discussion questions and extension suggestions to other picture books throughout the year. The more your students think about and practice conflict resolution, the better their social skills will develop. These improved skills can help promote a climate of peace in your classroom.

Feelings First

What Are Feelings?

Feelings lie at the base of conflict and confrontation. When in conflict, people often feel angry, afraid, frustrated, or confused. Recognizing and acknowledging these emotions is a primary step toward handling them appropriately. Children must be able to identify their feelings in order to express them in ways that promote understanding and peaceful conflict resolution. As children—and adults—come to realize and respect their own feelings, they will feel less threatened by others and more confident in managing their own reactions to conflict.

Feeling Faces

Use the reproducible on page 11 to help your students identify basic emotions and the impetus behind them. First, invite students to brainstorm and come up with a list of adjectives to describe their emotions. These might include the following:

happy	sad	excited	worried	sorry
proud	guilty	embarrassed	afraid	surprised
disappointed	impatient	silly	bored	tired
lonely	jealous	angry	content	loving

Give each student pencils, crayons, and a copy of the reproducible. Invite children to draw expressions on each face that represent the emotion listed beneath it. To extend the activity, have students choose one face and write a sentence on the back of the reproducible telling what might have caused the emotion. For example, beneath the face labeled *proud*, a student might write: "I felt proud when I won the race."

Monitor Emotions

Reinforce "emotion awareness." Each day, ask students to pause once or twice and identify how they are feeling at that moment. Leave a bowl of marbles, milk caps, or craft sticks on a table next to a series of jars labeled with emotions: happy, sad, worried, excited, and so on. Invite each student to place a marble, cap, or stick in the jar that corresponds with his or her feelings. Transfer results to a daily Feelings Graph: How many students were happy today? How many students felt worried or excited? Invite volunteers to share reasons behind their emotions. Is someone excited because a cousin is coming to visit? Worried about having forgotten a lunch box? Display the graphs on a bulletin board, along with explanations of the data ("More students felt happy than sad today," "Most of the class was excited on Friday," and so on).

Contributed by Sandra Thornburg
Metairie Park Country Day School
Metairie, Louisiana

Feeling Faces—Follow-Up Activities

☀ Play Card Games.

Have students cut along the dotted lines to make playing cards. Divide the class into small groups, and encourage them to use the Feeling Faces to play traditional card games such as Go Fish or Concentration.

☀ Play Feelings Bingo.

Ask students to cut along the dotted lines to separate the faces on the reproducible. Give each student an 8½- by 11-inch sheet of construction paper and some glue. Ask children to choose nine faces. To make a Bingo card, students should glue the faces onto the paper in three rows of three. Cut out one set of the faces for yourself and place them in a box or paper bag. Pick a square and call out the emotion on it (you can also make a facial expression to demonstrate the emotion). If a student has that emotion on his or her Bingo card, he or she covers the face with a chip, milk cap, or other manipulative. Play continues until someone has covered three faces in a row (vertically, horizontally, or diagonally).

☀ Make Feeling Puppets.

To make puppets, have students cut out the faces and glue them onto craft sticks. Students can work in small groups to create puppet shows that demonstrate various feelings.

☀ Feeling faces in action.

Ask students to make facial expressions that show how they would feel in various situations. Pause briefly after each sentence, so that students have a chance to show each different emotion. Here are some possible scenarios to read aloud:

Today is your birthday.　　　　　　　　There is a bee flying around your head.
Your birthday present gets lost.　　　　The bee lands on your arm.
You find it.　　　　　　　　　　　　It flies away.

(Adapted from an activity in *Resolving Conflict Creatively: A Teaching Guide for Grades K–8* by permission of the Board of Education of the city of New York.)

Where Do Feelings Come From?

Feelings come from inside a person, in response to stimuli such as thoughts, actions, or events. Ask your students to think of something that would cause them to feel surprised (a surprise birthday party or a package in the mail). Discuss why they would feel surprised: what happened was unexpected. Next, ask students to describe some things that might cause them to feel happy, sad, worried, afraid, angry, and so on. Help them understand that many things can affect emotions: events, words, actions, thoughts, books, movies, music, nature, and so on.

Teacher-Tested!

Puzzle Pairs

Create pairs of puzzle pieces that are identical in shape, color, and pattern. Mix them up and then give each student one piece. Ask children to study their puzzle piece and then find the classmate who holds its exact match. (The pieces do not have to fit together, but they must look alike.) Once partners have found each other, have them sit quietly until everyone has found a partner.

Ask a question that will bring an emotion to mind, such as "How would you feel if someone broke your favorite toy?" Have partners tell each other how they would feel in that situation. Then gather the class in a circle. Ask children to share their partner's response with the whole group. Discuss the variety of emotions people feel in a given situation.

Contributed by Jennifer Schedlbauer
Linden Avenue School
Glen Ridge, New Jersey

What Do Feelings Look Like?

Feelings evoke many responses in the body. They can make eyes widen, breathing quicken, and the heart beat faster. They can prompt laughter, tears, and goose bumps. Help students pinpoint signs of emotion in their bodies. Make a two-column chart on the chalkboard or on chart paper. Label the left column "Feelings" and the right column "What Happens?" List six or eight feelings in the left column. Ask students to tell you how their bodies feel as they experience each emotion. For example, ask "What does your body feel like when you're angry?" Students might report that their faces get hot, their hearts beat quickly, and their lungs feel tight. For "afraid," they might say their skin gets goose bumps, their mouths feel dry, and their hearts beat quickly.

NOTE: You might want to reproduce a small version of the chart and send it home with students. Ask them to pay attention to their bodies throughout the day and evening. When they experience one of the emotions listed, have them notice how their body responds and write it on the chart. Compile their findings the following day and add them to the class chart.

Feelings	What Happens?
angry	Face feels hot, heart beats quickly, lungs feel tight
afraid	Skin gets goose bumps, mouth feels dry, heart beats quickly

Make a Feelings Mini-Book

Encourage students to take a closer look at their own emotions by making a Feelings Mini-Book. Copy and distribute the reproducible on page 12. Demonstrate how to fold the paper as indicated to form a mini-book. Then walk children through the process of finishing the sentences and drawing pictures to go with them.

Make a Feelings Mini-Book—Follow-Up Activities

☼ In Living Color

Colors can evoke emotions and can also represent feelings. Help students understand

this connection through literature and song. Read aloud a picture book that connects feelings and colors, such as Dr. Seuss's *My Many Colored Days* (Knopf, 1996). You can also share singer Tom Chapin's "I've Got the Blues, Greens and Reds," an entertaining ballad about emotions in which a young child turns blue with disappointment, green with envy, and red with anger (Sony Kids' Music, 1992). Distribute paper and crayons or paint, and invite kids to use color to depict an emotion. Display the finished pieces and have students guess which emotion each drawing or painting represents.

☼ Play Feeling Charades.

Use index cards or small slips of paper to make emotion cards. On each card, write the name of an emotion (happy, disappointed, annoyed, and so on). Ask a volunteer to choose a card and act out the emotion written on it. Explain that, rather than using words, children should act out the emotion through facial expressions and body language—for example, by frowning, yawning, or jumping up and down.

☼ Hung Up on Feelings

Ask each student to bring in a wire hanger, a nylon stocking or sock, and any scraps of ribbon, yarn, felt, or other fabric they wish. Provide glue and movable eyes. Bend the bottom of the hanger to form a more circular face. Have students stretch the nylon to fit over the hanger, making the face, as shown. Let students glue on eyes and other facial features so that the expression reflects a specific emotion such as joy, anger, or surprise. To display the faces, simply hang them up!

Feeling Faces

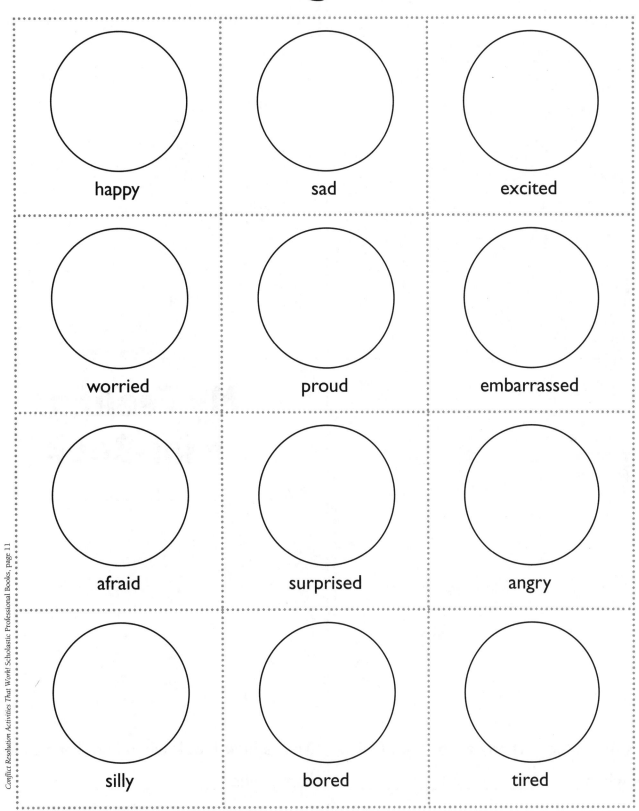

happy

sad

excited

worried

proud

embarrassed

afraid

surprised

angry

silly

bored

tired

This is how I look when I am proud. I feel proud when ______________________

____

3

This is how I look when I am sad. I feel sad when ______________________

____

2

1. First, fold along this line.

My Feelings Mini-Book

by ______________________________________

2. Next, fold along this line.

This is how I look when I am angry. I feel angry when ______________________

____

4

This is how I look when I am happy. I feel happy when ______________________

____

1

Preventing and Responding to Conflict

Conflict Resolution Is a Process

Conflict resolution does not offer any quick or easy solutions. It is an ongoing process of learning. Everyone has the tools to resolve conflicts peacefully, but most children have not had enough experience using them. That is the purpose of this book: to give kids the opportunity to practice responding effectively to conflict when it arises. By teaching children a variety of strategies to work through disagreements, you are helping them promote peace, respect, and understanding.

When discussing conflict resolution strategies with children, William J. Kreidler suggests first using concrete terms (such as specific behaviors) and later moving on to more abstract ideas (such as point of view). He emphasizes the importance of discussing cause and effect, a key concept in conflict resolution. Kreidler recommends guiding children to understand that their actions have consequences and that there are many approaches to resolving a conflict, not just one (*Teaching Conflict Resolution Through Children's Literature*, page 8).

Promote a Peaceful Environment

Discuss the following actions with children. Encourage them to think about how these simple actions can foster positive relationships and a peaceful environment.

☼ Speak and act with kindness.

In times of conflict, kind words and actions often vanish in favor of harsh ones. Build students' repertoire of kind words, and encourage them to avoid saying words that are

hurtful to others. Get students in the habit of speaking kindly, so that kind words become more automatic than unkind ones. Applaud good-hearted gestures, compliments, and helpful behaviors as they happen, and it's likely they will happen more and more.

☀ Reach out to others.

Compassion blooms where it's planted. Encourage students to show empathy toward their classmates. Acknowledge those who accompany injured classmates to the nurse, ask a sad classmate if they can help, or otherwise care for the needs and feelings of others.

☀ Treat others with respect.

Explain to students that the way we treat others is likely to affect the way we are treated in return. Those who speak and act kindly can expect the same; those who step on others' feelings have little recourse when their own feelings are hurt.

☀ Understand and respect other points of view.

No two people view every situation in exactly the same way. Conflicts often escalate because people refuse to regard other points of view as valid or feel threatened when others don't agree. Help your students understand that they need not be upset when others don't see things their way.

☀ Work and play cooperatively.

Practice makes perfect, and no activity gives students more practice at getting along than cooperative play. Putting students in small groups to solve problems, play games, and complete projects reinforces cooperation and communication—two key players in conflict prevention and resolution.

Be an Active Listener

Effective communication lies at the heart of preventing and resolving conflict. Discuss with children what it means to communicate effectively. Explain that communication involves both speaking and listening. Ask children if they can think of ways to be a good listener, and write their ideas on chart paper or on the chalkboard. Promote active listening in your classroom by sharing and role-playing these guidelines:

☀ Focus your attention on the speaker. Stop what you are doing and look at the person speaking.

☼ Acknowledge that you understand. Nod your head or respond briefly ("Uh-huh . . . I see . . .") from time to time to let the speaker know that you are listening.

☼ Try not to interrupt. Interrupting may cause the speaker to lose his or her train of thought. It is also impolite.

☼ Paraphrase when appropriate. Repeat in your own words the speaker's ideas or message. ("So you feel angry because Paul left your crayons in the sun and now they've melted?")

☼ Avoid solving the problem for the speaker, unless you are asked to do so. You might ask questions ("What do you think you should do about it?") or simply let the conversation continue until the speaker solves the problem. ("You're going to let Paul know that you'll only lend your things to him if he promises to care of them? Sounds good to me.")

Teacher-Tested!

Complimentary Quilts

Make compliments commonplace in your classroom with this easy activity. Each week, choose one student and ask classmates to think of something they appreciate about that child. Compliments might include "Jared walks quietly in line" or "Jared is helpful. He picked up my pencil when I dropped it." Give each student an 8- by 8-inch square of paper. Have students write their compliment at the bottom of the page and draw an illustration to go with it. Glue the pictures in rows on a large sheet of craft paper. Hang the complimentary quilt in the classroom for the rest of the week, and then send it home as a keepsake for the student who is the subject of the quilt.

Hint: Eliminate student anticipation by assigning each student a week during which he or she will be the subject of a complimentary quilt. Determine the order alphabetically, or let students pick numbers during the first week of school. Then post a calendar that lets students know when they will be the subject of the quilt.

Contributed by Cheryl Coderre
Father John V. Doyle School
Coventry, Rhode Island

Dare to Care!

☼ Dare to care!

Set up a Caring Squad in your classroom—in which everyone is a member! Make squad membership cards, and encourage members to watch for caring acts in the classroom and beyond. When a squad member witnesses a caring act, have that person write a sentence about it in a Caring Squad Logbook (a decorated notebook

placed in a prominent spot in the classroom). At the end of each week, read aloud from the logbook, applauding the efforts of the squad. At the end of each month, hold a squad celebration of some kind. One month, students may enjoy an ice cream treat. Another month, they may perform a kind act for another class or an individual.

☀ Agree or disagree?

Help students see that people don't always view situations in the same way. Stand before the class and state an opinion about something, such as "Spring is the best season of the year." Ask students who agree with the statement to stand on the left side of the room. Ask students who disagree to stand on the right side. Ask students who are unsure to stand in the center. Invite students to tell why they agree with the statement, disagree with it, or are unsure. Then try the exercise again, using a different statement. Be sure to stress the point that you are asking for students' opinions and that there are no right or wrong answers.

⋆ Teacher-Tested! ⋆

Textile Words

Some words are soft and soothing to the listener, while others are abrasive and rough. This activity gives students a hands-on experience with the "texture" of words. To help teach the concept of positive and negative language, cover one block of wood with velvet and another with sandpaper. As children feel the textures and talk about how words can feel like velvet or sandpaper, they come to understand how their own words can be comforting or abrasive to others.

Contributed by Sharon Atkinson
Riviera Beach Elementary School
Pasadena, Maryland

This activity appeared in *Instructor* magazine, May/June 1996.

Know How to Respond to Conflict

When a conflict arises, students need to know that there are many ways to deal with it. Review the suggestions listed below with your students. Then display the suggestions in the classroom so students can refer to them as needed. The following tactics may be useful in resolving classroom conflicts:

☀ Let both sides win.

Encourage students to look for win-win solutions (ways to solve a problem that meet the needs of everyone involved). To do this, students must study the problem and identify the needs of each person. For example, Will's coat hook is just below Jan's. Every day, Jan hangs her coat, umbrella, and backpack on her hook. Will can barely find his hook below Jan's, and her belongings often slip off the hook and fall on him. The problem: Jan and Will have a small space and need to find a way they can both use it. Their needs: Jan needs a place to store her belongings; Will needs clear access to a hook. What is the solution? Jan might put her backpack on the floor and slide her umbrella inside it, or Will and Jan might work together, using the bottom hook for coats and umbrellas and the top for both backpacks. In either case, the solution meets both of their needs.

☀ Use I-messages.

Each person states how he or she feels about the situation and explains what he or she needs or wants (assertive behavior). No one is allowed to be rough or forceful (aggressive behavior), yet no one is encouraged to retreat (passive behavior). For additional information on I-messages, see pages 18–20.

☀ Talk it out.

Each person lets the other speak without interruption. Both parties are encouraged to listen carefully in order to understand what the other thinks and feels.

☀ Put the conflict on hold.

When tempers are high, cooling off is often the best solution. Both parties need to walk away from each other and discuss the conflict at another time.

☀ Avoid blaming and verbal assault.

Blaming or insulting escalates conflict and halts communication. The people involved must express their needs and feelings, applying energy toward solving the problem rather than venting anger toward another person.

☀ Apologize.

A well-meant apology can go a long way toward solving a conflict.

☼ Seek help when it's needed.

When peacemaking tactics don't work, find an adult or peer to mediate. Mediators should allow each person to express his or her feelings without judging them. Rather than dictating a solution, the mediator works with those in conflict to find a suitable solution.

☼ Share and take turns.

Both people agree to equal time with the desired toy or object.

☼ Compromise.

Both people give in a little for the sake of peace.

✦ Use I-Messages ✦

Being assertive means standing up for yourself and telling others how you feel and what you want to happen. One way to do this effectively is to use I-messages. Like anything else, using I-messages can feel strange at first. With repeated use, it can become second nature. Below are several useful patterns for stating I-messages. Share them with your students, and encourage them to use these examples as models for their own.

1. I feel _____ when you _____
           (how you feel)   (what person is doing)

because _____ .
                          (why it bothers you)

Example:
"I feel hurt when you call me carrot top because it sounds like you're making fun of my hair."

2. I _____ when you _____
      (don't like it/don't appreciate it)   (what person is doing)

because _____ .
                  (tell why it bothers you)

Example:
"I don't appreciate it when you draw on my desk because it makes my desk messy."

3. I _____ when you _____
      (don't like it/don't appreciate it)   (what person is doing)

and I would like _____.

(what you would like to happen)

Example:

"I don't like it when you borrow my crayons without asking, and I would like you to ask me next time."

Duplicate and hand out the reproducible on page 30. Complete the first two examples as a class in order to give students a clear idea of how to form their own I-messages.

Use I-Messages—Follow-Up Activities

☀ Practice I-Messaging.

Discourage the use of accusing statements, such as "You're always pushing people." Instead, encourage children to use assertive I-messages, such as "I don't like being pushed. Please stop pushing me."

☀ Reenact Classroom Conflicts.

Divide the class into small groups of three to four students. Have each group choose a common conflict and act it out for classmates in two different scenarios. In the first scenario, ask students to solve the problem in an ineffective manner (doing nothing about it, feeling angry with one another, and so on). In the second scenario, ask students to handle the problem assertively, by standing up for themselves and expressing their needs and wants. Examples of conflict might include two students wanting to play with the same jump rope, two students leaving a third one out of play, or two students disagreeing on the rules for a board game.

☀ Make an Interactive Bulletin Board.

Create a classroom display that reminds students to use I-messages. Here's how:

1. Cut eight identical turtle shapes, approximately 3 by 5 inches, from posterboard.

2. Write a conflict on each turtle, such as "Someone is talking too loud" or "Someone does not want to share."

3. Cut out a separate posterboard shell for each turtle, large enough to cover the conflict.

4. On each shell, write an effective message to handle one of the conflicts, such as "Please talk softer. Loud voices hurt my ears." or "I'd like a turn with that ball. May I have it next?"

5. Attach a small square of Velcro to each turtle body and to the back of each shell.

6. Cut a two-foot length of yarn for each turtle shell.

7. Staple one end of the yarn to the turtle shell and the other end to the center of the bulletin board, so that the string can reach any of the eight messages.

8. Invite students to use the bulletin board during free time. Explain that the task is to cover each conflict with an effective response.

Conflict Story Strips

Like comic strips, story strips tell stories through words and pictures. They are called story strips rather than comic strips because they explore situations that are serious rather than comical. Story strips are an appealing medium for students to explore—and kids will

enjoy creating their own. Use the first reproducible, Lucas and Soun (page 31), to provide practice in reading and understanding story strips. Then hand out the Make Your Own Story Strip reproducible (page 32) to guide students as they create their own tales of conflict and resolution.

Copy and distribute the reproducible, and then read through the story strips with students. Invite them to tell what is happening in each scene, and help them identify the conflict. Then ask them to tell which response worked best and why. Guide students to understand that in every conflict, people can choose how they will respond. They can respond

with aggressive behavior (hitting, shouting, blaming, and name-calling), passive behavior (doing nothing), or assertive behavior (telling others how they feel and what they want others to do). Explain that the story strips show three different ways Lucas might have responded when Soun cut in front of him. Talk about the consequences of each: aggressive behavior resulted in physical injury, passive behavior resulted in lowering Lucas's self-esteem, and assertive behavior resulted in increasing Lucas's confidence about handling problems.

✶ What's Happening Here? ✶

Copy and distribute the reproducible on page 33. Give students time to study the pictures. Then talk about each one, using the questions below as springboards for discussion. Explain that the pictures are open to interpretation and that there are no right or wrong answers.

Ask students to tell what they see in picture A: What is the boy doing? What is the girl doing? How are they each feeling, and how can students tell they are feeling this way? Then ask students to speculate about the details surrounding the picture. Was the boy using the ball and then the girl decided to take it away from him? Did the girl and the boy agree that they would each get a turn with the ball, and now the boy won't give her a turn? How else can the girl get a turn without grabbing the ball? Examining the conflict in this way will help students understand the emotions the children are feeling. This will make it easier for students to come up with a peaceful solution to the problem.

Next, invite students to explore what is happening in picture B. What are the children doing? What has happened to one boy's picture? How are both boys feeling? Why are they feeling this way? Invite students to speculate. Who spilled the paint? Was it spilled by accident or on purpose? How do children think the conflict can be resolved peacefully?

What's Happening Here?—Follow-Up Activities

☼ Guess What's Happening?

Let students draw their own conflict scenes and explain them to the class. You might also have children draw conflicts and let classmates guess what is going on in each picture. Give students the opportunity to discuss ways in which the conflicts could be resolved.

☼ Look at pictures or photographs that depict conflict.

In picture books, magazines, or newspapers, look for pictures or photographs that show conflict. Examining and discussing these images can reinforce students' understanding of various conflicts. Show one picture or photograph to the class and ask questions, such as: "What do you think the conflict is about? How do you think the people involved feel? How can the conflict be resolved?" Divide the class into groups and give each group one or more images to discuss. When groups are finished, they can share their ideas about their pictures with the rest of the class.

Build a Conflict Cube

Put peacemaking skills at your students' fingertips with Conflict Cubes they can make themselves. Here's how:

1. Give each student a copy of the reproducible on page 34.

2. In each square, have students illustrate each of the ways listed to resolve and avoid conflict: use I-messages, talk things out, take time to cool off, listen carefully, reach a compromise, and treat others with respect.

3. Show students how to assemble a cube by cutting, folding, and taping the edges together.

TAPE EDGES

Build a Conflict Cube—Follow-Up Activities

☼ What Will I Do?

Divide the class into small groups. Invite group members to invent conflict scenarios, such as "Jessica spilled milk on your desk and won't clean it up. What will you do?" One at a time, group members roll their story boxes and respond by using the strategy that is shown on top. (A child who rolls "Use I-messages" might say, "I don't like having milk spilled on my desk because my papers will get wet. Please help me clean it up.")

☼ Roll a Story.

Have students roll their cubes and write, draw, or act out stories based on what lands on top. For example, their stories might be about someone listening carefully or treating someone else with respect.

☼ Use Cubes to Resolve Conflicts.

Encourage students to solve mild conflicts by rolling a Conflict Cube and using the strategy that appears on top.

Spin a Listening Wheel

Of all the skills students will need to prevent and resolve conflicts, listening is one of the most important. When people truly listen, they are better able to understand different points of view and see other sides to a story. They notice the needs and wants of another person. Sometimes this is enough to avert or help solve a conflict.

As mentioned on pages 14–15, active listening requires a few basic skills. Share the following primary version of these skills with your students, demonstrating what each entails and guiding them in practice:

☼ Look at the speaker.

☼ Be still and quiet.

☼ Let one person speak at a time.

☼ Pay attention.

☼ Make eye contact with the speaker.

☼ Use body language to show that you are listening.

☼ Try not to interrupt.

☼ Accept the other person's feelings without judging.

☼ Paraphrase to be sure you understand.

Give each student a copy of the Listening Wheel reproducible on page 35. Help children follow these directions to assemble their wheels:

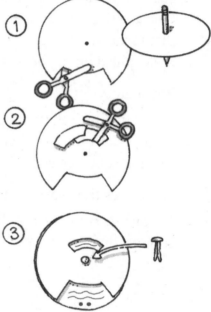

1. Cut out the wheels. Use a hole punch or pencil to make holes in the center of the wheels. (Note: Remind children to be careful if using a pencil to poke the hole.)

2. Cut out the window in wheel A. (To make cutting easier, fold the wheel in half.)

3. Place wheel A on top of wheel B. Attach the two wheels with a brass fastener. Let students experiment with turning their wheels and reading the statements about listening. Then lead a group discussion about listening skills. Model good listening skills for your students, and remind children to use them in group discussions, assemblies, and whenever necessary.

★ *Teacher-Tested!* ★

Pass the Power Ball!

Encourage active listening by inviting students to sit cross-legged in a circle. Hold a tennis ball or other small ball in your hand, and explain to students that it is the "Speaker Power Ball." When someone holds the power ball, he or she is the only person allowed to speak; everyone else must listen. To reinforce the power ball concept, hold the ball in your hand and make a statement, such as "My favorite color is blue." Then pass the ball to the student on your left. Ask that student to name his or her favorite color and pass the ball. Continue around the circle until the ball returns to you. Then make a different statement and pass the ball again, inviting students to follow suit. To check listening skills, pause now and then and ask students to tell what a previous student has said. Once students have the idea, you can use the power ball anytime to encourage children to listen to each other.

Contributed by Jennifer Schedlbauer
Linden Avenue School
Glen Ridge, New Jersey

See More Sides Than One

As mentioned earlier, preventing and resolving conflict involves realizing and accepting that people have different viewpoints. For young children, this concept can be difficult to comprehend. When embroiled in conflict, children often cling to their side of the story and refuse to accept or even acknowledge someone else's point of view. The following activities will help students develop awareness and acceptance of diverse viewpoints.

Give each student a copy of the reproducible on page 36. Have children color and cut out the two circles. Then demonstrate how to glue them back to back. Explain to children that people often see the same event in different ways. Ask students to identify the event on side A (rainfall) and tell how the boy in the picture feels about the rain. Then ask them to identify the event on side B (rainfall) and tell how the girl in the picture feels about the rain. Explain the expression "There are two sides to every coin." Invite students to tell about other times when they have viewed an event differently than someone else. Invite them to use their two-sided coins as a reminder that others may see things differently— and that it's okay.

See More Sides Than One—Follow-Up Activities

The following activities will help reinforce the point-of-view concept.

☼ Read a story that gives an unusual slant to a popular fairy tale, such as *The True Story of the Three Little Pigs* by Jon Scieszka (Viking Kestrel, 1989), *The Frog Prince, Continued* by Jon Scieszka (Viking, 1991), or *The Three Little Wolves and the Big Bad Pig* by Eugene Trivizas (Margaret K. McElderry Books, 1993). Discuss how the main character in each story is portrayed in the original version of the tale. You may wish to make a chart to record the differences between the original version of the tale and the remake.

☀ Read aloud a popular fairy tale or picture book, such as Goldilocks and the Three Bears. Call on volunteers to pretend to act as the various characters in the story. Invite classmates to interview the characters to find out how they feel about the main events in the story.

☀ Write stories or draw pictures from the point of view of an insect, mouse, bird, fish, or other small creature. Present various situations and ask students to describe the creature's point of view. For example, a family wants to get a mouse out of their house. How does the mouse feel?

Puppet Play

Puppets are a great way to help children adjust to new situations, express their feelings, and work through difficult situations. Puppets also offer a fun approach to exploring conflict resolution. With puppets, children can hone their communication skills and try new ways of responding to conflict, before they actually put them into practice.

Here are some tips on puppet play:

☀ Sometimes students will use their puppets to hit or bite. Before puppet playtime, model appropriate use of hand puppets.

☀ Provide a puppet theater. Even a card table draped with a tablecloth can create a theatrical atmosphere, encouraging creativity and freedom of expression.

☀ Let students make their own puppets using craft sticks, glue, felt, construction paper, and various accessories (movable eyes, glitter, yarn, sequins, beads, buttons, and so on).

Encourage students to use the puppets independently or in small groups, during free time or scheduled class time. Have students use puppets to resolve actual conflicts that happen during the school day.

From time to time, pick up a puppet during group time and pretend it is a visitor to your classroom. Have the puppet explain a problem he or she is experiencing and ask the class

for suggestions to resolve it.

Give each student a copy of the reproducibles on pages 37–38. The first sheet offers suggestions for puppet show themes. Students may wish to choose a theme from the list or come up with their own. The second provides templates for six puppets. Demonstrate how to color, cut out, and glue the puppets onto craft sticks. They can then use these puppets in their shows.

Puppet Play—Follow-Up Activities

After children have performed a puppet play, lead a discussion about it with the class. You might also have the performers lead the discussion. If desired, students can have the puppets ask questions of the class. For example, students can ask how the audience thought a character felt during a particular part of the puppet show. They can ask the audience to evaluate how the conflict was resolved and to offer alternate strategies.

Make a Story Mover

Let students use the reproducible on page 39 to create and display their own conflict and resolution stories. Here's how:

1. Give each student a copy of the reproducible. Help them cut out the story strip along the dotted lines.

2. Help students cut along the two dotted lines inside the story frame.

3. Demonstrate how to insert the story strip in the frame. Pull it along to show students how to use it.

4. Have each student take the story strip out of the frame and draw three or four scenes on it to depict both the conflict and its resolution. The story can be real or imaginary, and the conflict need not be elaborate. It can be as basic as two boys

tugging on a block, talking about what to do, and then using the block to build a tower together. Students may wish to use the first box as a title page.

Place the Story Movers within students' reach to make an interactive display they can use during free time.

Read-Aloud Play: Trouble on the Playground

At the base of many conflicts lies misunderstanding. Often, words or actions that were never intended as hurtful are perceived that way when someone misunderstands another's intention. Without proper communication, a conflict that starts in this way can blow out of proportion quickly and be difficult to resolve.

When people express their feelings calmly and listen carefully to one another, disagreements and hurt feelings can change to harmonious interaction, as both parties realize their needs and emotions are being taken into account.

The read-aloud play "Trouble on the Playground" (pages 40–43) highlights a simple and typical misunderstanding that results in discord between friends. Invite volunteers to act out the play. You may want to have students read through the play on their own first, so that they can anticipate the emotions of their characters.

Read-Aloud Play—Follow-Up Activities

☼ Take Two!

Invite students to think of an alternative to the events in the play. For example, the characters could come together soon after the argument happens instead of days later. How would this have affected the outcome of the story? Students can write out a new scene for the play, or role-play in small groups.

☀ Apply Conflict Resolution Techniques.

Divide the class into small groups. Assign each group a resolution technique from the conflict cube. (See the reproducible on page 34.) Have students reenact a portion of the play that demonstrates use of that resolution skill or revise any portion of the script to reflect the skill.

☀ Start a Story Strip.

Make a conflict story strip based on the play. (See the reproducible on page 32.)

☀ Act With Puppets.

Turn the play into a puppet show. Have children create puppets to represent characters in the play. They can also create scenery for the playground, classroom, and bus.

☀ Draw an Audience.

Perform the play for parents or other classes in the school. Help the children rehearse their lines and create scenery. Find a job that fits each child in your class—such as acting, set production, operating lights or music, creating programs, or presenting a brief introduction or wrap-up to highlight what your class has learned about conflict resolution techniques.

Use I-Messages

Read each sentence below. Write an I-message for each.

1 Jean borrowed Kira's markers and forgot to return them. What could Kira say to Jean?

_____

_____

_____

_____

2 Joe wants to play soccer with Rahim and no one else. Rahim wants his other friends to play, too. What could Rahim say to Joe?

_____

_____

_____

_____

3 Kim is bouncing a ball. Carlos keeps trying to take it from her. What could Kim say to Carlos?

_____

_____

_____

_____

_____

Lucas and Soun

Aggressive

Passive

Assertive

Make Your Own Story Strip

Aggressive

Passive

Assertive

What's Happening Here?

A

B

Build a Conflict Cube

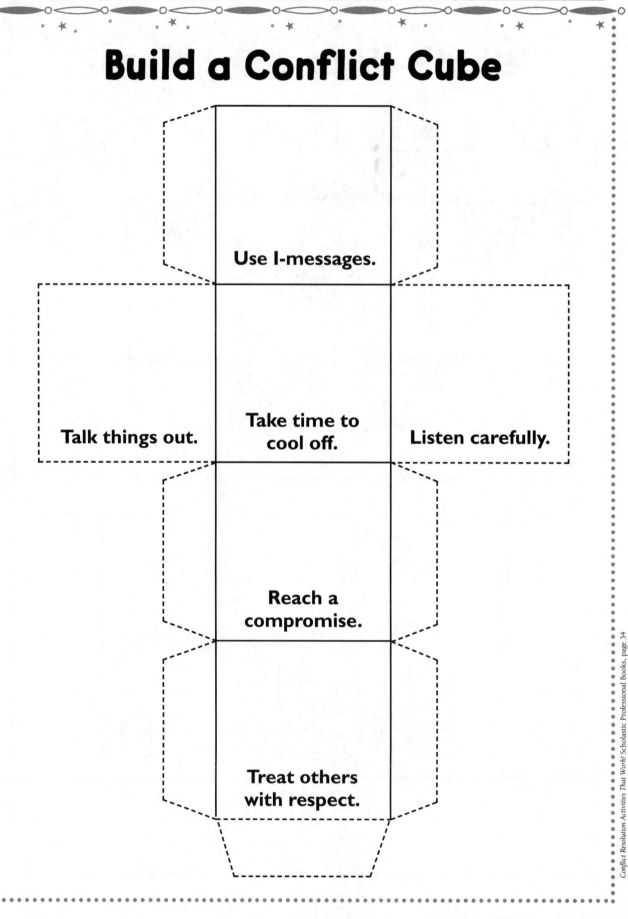

Use I-messages.

Talk things out.   **Take time to cool off.**   **Listen carefully.**

Reach a compromise.

Treat others with respect.

Spin a Listening Wheel

Wheel A

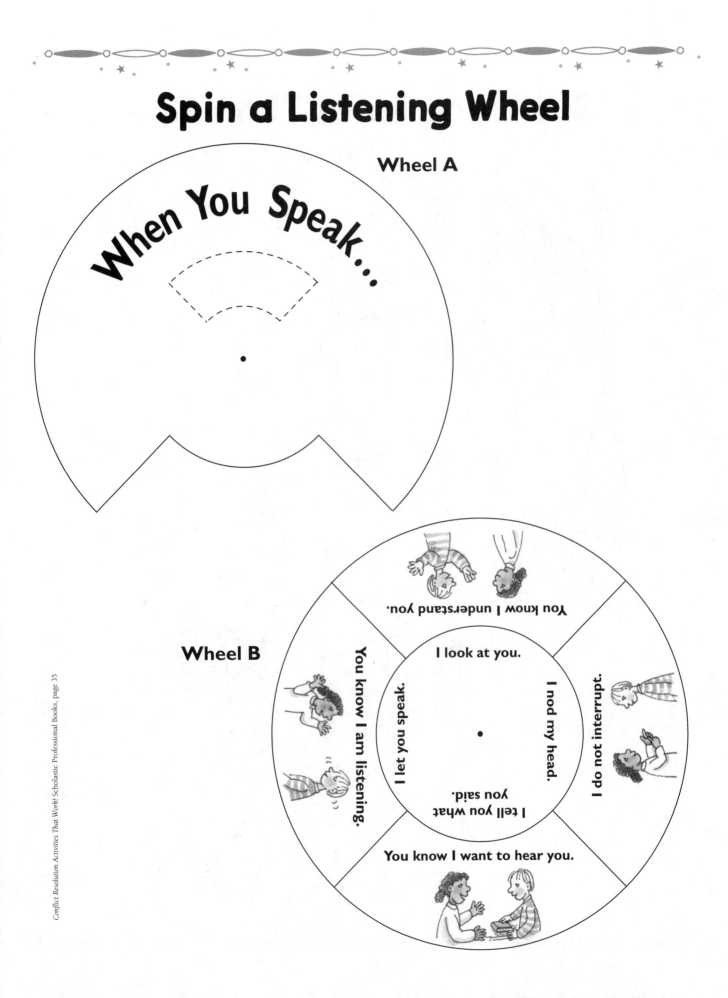

When You Speak...

Wheel B

I look at you.

You know I understand you.

I do not interrupt.

I nod my head.

I tell you what you said.

You know I want to hear you.

You know I am listening.

I let you speak.

See More Sides Than One

Side A

Side B

Puppet Play

Here are some ideas you can use for your puppet show:

☀ A friend borrows your favorite toy and breaks it.

☀ Your mom asks you to take out the dog again, but it's really your sister's turn.

☀ Your brother eats all but one piece of your bubble gum.

☀ Your friend leaves your favorite book out in the rain.

☀ You and your friend want to use the same toy at the same time.

☀ You are working in a group, and one child is acting bossy.

☀ Some classmates have been teasing you at school.

☀ Your best friend shared her candy with everyone but you.

☀ It's your turn for the swing, and another child won't get off.

☀ A friend borrowed a dollar and forgot to pay you back.

☀ A girl in your class calls you a nickname that you don't like.

☀ You accidentally bump into someone and knock him or her down. Now that person is angry.

☀ Your mom is upset because you teased your brother and made him cry.

☀ Your dad wants you to clean your room now, but you would rather read.

Puppet Play

Directions: Color, cut out, and glue the characters below onto craft sticks.

Make a Story Mover

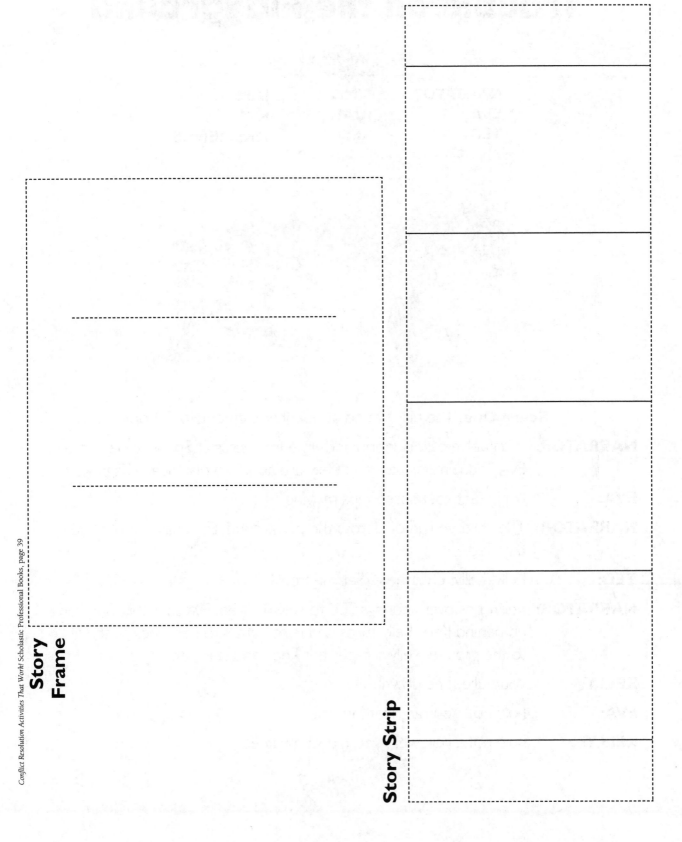

**Story
Frame**

Story Strip

Read-Aloud Play
Trouble on the Playground

★ Characters ★

NARRATOR	**SIMON**	**JAN**
EVA	**JUAN**	**KIM**
TED	**KELLY**	**MRS. JENKS**

Scene One: The playground at Spencer Elementary School

NARRATOR: It is twelve o'clock noon and time for recess at Spencer Elementary. Eva, Ted, Simon, Juan, and Kelly are about to play Space Tag.

EVA: I'm it. Get your spaceships moving!

NARRATOR: The children run off across the playground. Eva chases them and tags Ted.

TED: Kelly! Kelly! Over here! Set me free!

NARRATOR: Kelly runs over and tags Ted to set him free. Eva sees this. She runs up behind Kelly. Kelly turns and runs right into her. They both fall to the ground. Kelly scrapes her knee and starts to cry.

KELLY: You pulled me down!

EVA: I did not! You ran right into me!

KELLY: I did not. Look what you did to my knee!

Conflict Resolution Activities That Work! Scholastic Professional Books

EVA:	You should watch where you're going, you big crybaby.
KELLY:	(*Stops crying.*) You're mean, Eva, and you're not my friend anymore.
EVA:	Who wants to be friends with you anyway? (*Eva walks away.*)
NARRATOR:	Ted helps Kelly get up. Juan and Simon walk over.
JUAN:	What happened? Are we still playing Space Tag?
KELLY:	We're still playing, but Eva's not. She hurts people and she doesn't even care.
SIMON:	I'm it!
NARRATOR:	Ted, Kelly, Juan, and Simon run off. Eva walks to the wall of the school and sits down. She feels like crying.
EVA:	I'm not going to be a crybaby, like Kelly. She's so mean to me. I don't like her anymore.
NARRATOR:	Jan and Kim walk over to Eva.
JAN:	Eva, we need a third person for jump rope. Want to play?
EVA:	Okay.

Scene Two: The classroom

NARRATOR:	Recess ends, and the class goes inside. On the way in the door, Eva and Kelly give each other nasty looks. For the rest of the school day, they do not look at each other.
MRS. JENKS:	Okay, children. Please get your backpacks and line up at the door.
NARRATOR:	Eva and Kelly end up standing next to each other in line.

KELLY:	Your backpack is bumping into me.
EVA:	Move up, then.
KELLY:	I was here first. You move.
EVA:	I guess I'd better, or you'll knock me down again.
KELLY:	I told you, I didn't knock you down. It was all your fault.
NARRATOR:	Eva and Kelly go home without saying anything else to each other. They sit in separate seats on the bus. For the first time in weeks, they do not play together after school.

Scene Three: The school bus

NARRATOR:	The next morning, Kelly wants to try to make things right. She sees Eva get on the bus.
KELLY:	Eva! Sit with me!
NARRATOR:	Eva glares at Kelly and walks by without speaking. Kelly shrinks back into her seat. She feels sad and lonely. At the next stop, Ted and Juan get on. They sit near Eva.
TED:	Why aren't you sitting with Kelly today?
EVA:	She was mean to me yesterday. I don't want to sit with her.
TED:	It was an accident. I saw what happened.
EVA:	I didn't pull her down.
TED:	I know. She didn't push you, either.
JUAN:	Remember what Mrs. Jenks told us. We need to talk things out when there's trouble.
TED:	You and Kelly need to talk.

NARRATOR:	At school, Ted and Juan talk with Mrs. Jenks. They tell her what happened on the playground yesterday. Mrs. Jenks calls Kelly and Eva to her desk.
MRS. JENKS:	Girls, Ted and Juan told me what happened yesterday. They think it would be a good idea if you two talked about it. How about going to the Work-It-Out Table?
NARRATOR:	Kelly and Eva sit at the Work-It-Out Table in the back of the room. For a few minutes, they don't say anything. They don't know what to say.
EVA:	(*Quietly*) I didn't pull you down yesterday. I was going to tag you, but I didn't get close enough.
KELLY:	I was angry because I thought you pulled me down.
EVA:	When you yelled at me, I felt angry, too. I would never pull you down on purpose.
KELLY:	I didn't know you were behind me. I must have bumped into you.
EVA:	I guess we should have talked things out yesterday.
KELLY:	I'm sorry I yelled at you.
EVA:	I'm sorry I yelled at you, too.
KELLY:	I didn't mean it when I said you weren't my friend. You are my friend, Eva.
EVA:	I'm glad you said that, because it's no fun without you.
KELLY:	Do you want to play with me at recess?
EVA:	Yes, but let's not play Space Tag this time!

THE END

Conflict Resolution Activities That Work! Scholastic Professional Books

Exploring Conflict Resolution Through Reading and Writing

Exploring Conflict Through Children's Literature

Children's books provide a wonderful segue into discussing conflict and conflict resolution. The books in this section represent just a few of the many excellent choices for exploring the topics of emotions, communication, respect, and more. Whenever you read a story to the class, ask them to talk about how the characters felt at different points of the story, how they handled their emotions, and so on. You can also ask them to think of alternate methods of resolving the conflict in the story. These kinds of questions strengthen their reading comprehension skills and their conflict resolution skills.

Chrysanthemum—Introducing the Story

Chrysanthemum by Kevin Henkes (Greenwillow, 1991)
Synopsis: A young mouse's first days in kindergarten are clouded when classmates make fun of her name.

Learning Points:

☀ Teasing can hurt others' feelings.

☀ It is important to treat others with respect.

☀ Appreciate yourself, even if others don't.

Before reading the story, invite children to tell what it means to tease someone and how it feels to be teased. Emphasize that teasing can be hurtful even if it is only intended to be

playful. Help children understand that teasing someone—whether it is about hair color, height, clothing, accent, abilities, or any other personal characteristic—can be painful and cruel, even if they don't mean for it to be.

✷ **Exploring the Story** ✷

Read *Chrysanthemum* aloud to students. Invite students to tell how Chrysanthemum felt about her name before she went to school. Then talk about how Chrysanthemum felt after her classmates giggled at her name and talked about her on the playground.

✷ *Chrysanthemum—Follow-Up Activities* ✷

✵ Confidence Blooms Where It's Planted!

Distribute paper, pencils, and crayons. Ask each child to draw a daisy with six petals. Then ask children to think about the skills or attributes they possess that they are proud of. Inside each petal, have children write one attribute or skill—for example, "I like to share," "I can run fast," or "Friends can count on me."

✵ Take Second Chances.

Invite each student to think about a time when he or she teased someone else or was teased by someone else. Have students reflect on this incident, recalling how they or the person they teased felt. Distribute paper and pencils, and ask students to either write about or draw the scene. Then ask them to write about or draw a different version of the incident, this time leaving out the teasing. Encourage them to contrast the two scenarios and the feelings of the people involved in each.

✵ Rewrite It!

Help students rewrite a popular fairy tale (or a scene from a fairy tale). In their versions, encourage students to have characters employ nonaggressive means to prevent or resolve conflict. For example, Papa Bear might use an I-message instead of roaring when he finds Goldilocks asleep upstairs. When confronted, Goldilocks might apologize and offer to repair the damage. Students might enjoy rewriting the following stories, among others: Chicken Little, Goldilocks and the Three Bears, The Little Red Hen, The Three Billy Goats Gruff, and The Three Little Pigs.

Boy, Can He Dance!—Introducing the Story

Boy, Can He Dance! by Eileen Spinelli (Four Winds Press, 1993)
Synopsis: A young boy tries to follow in his father's footsteps, but his own feet—and heart—lead him in a different direction.

Learning Points:

☼ Believe in yourself, even when others doubt you.

☼ Appreciate and respect differences.

Explain that you are going to read a story about a boy who loved to do something and followed his dream, despite what others wanted. Before reading the book, ask children to think about something they love to do. How do they feel when they are doing this activity? Ask children to describe to a partner the activity and their feelings about it.

Exploring the Story

Invite students to tell how Tony felt when he danced. Then talk about how Tony felt when he worked in the kitchen. Why did Tony's father want him to be a chef? Help students explore the chaos that resulted when Tony tried to be who his father wanted him to be instead of finding a place to do what he wanted—to dance.

Boy, Can He Dance!—Follow-Up Activities

☼ Draw a Positive Self-Portrait.

Have children each draw a self-portrait and then draw six lines extending from their head. On each line, have students write one skill or positive attribute they possess.

☼ Make a Classroom Yellow Pages.

Invite each child to think of a skill or interest he or she possesses that might be useful to the class. A student might be skillful at math, reading, running, drawing, singing, dancing, acting, leading a group, making others smile, and so on. Ask students to draw themselves performing their particular skill. Then have them

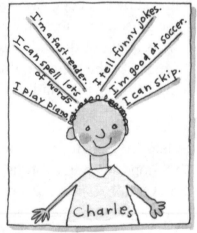

write a sentence or two to describe the skill, such as "I can help others with math." Compile the pages to make a Classroom Yellow Pages for children to refer to when they need to find someone to help them—or when they want to feel proud of themselves!

☀ Together, We Can!

Invite children to share with the class something they enjoy doing or something they do well. They could demonstrate a sports skill, display a structure they've built, sing a song, and so on. If a camera is available, photograph each student performing or displaying his or her skill. Tack the photos to a bulletin board entitled "Together, We Can Do It All!"

Ruby the Copycat—Introducing the Story

Ruby the Copycat by Peggy Rathmann (Scholastic, 1991)
Synopsis: A newcomer, Ruby tries to make friends by copying those she admires. She soon learns that copying can hurt others and that it's best to be yourself.

Learning Points:

☀ Be yourself.

☀ Look for the good that is inside of people.

Discuss what it means to copy someone else. Ask students when it is okay to copy, such as when playing Follow the Leader or writing down a homework assignment. Then ask when copying is not appropriate. For example, it is not okay to tease someone by mimicking her words or facial expressions. It is also not acceptable to copy someone else's answers on a test.

Exploring the Story

Read the story aloud. Ask students why Ruby copied Angela (because she felt insecure being new at school, she felt she didn't have anything exciting of her own to offer the class, she admired Angela's beautiful bows and clothing, and so on). Invite students to study the illustrations, noting the expressions on Ruby's and Angela's faces at various points in the story, such as when Ruby admires Angela's bow, when Angela feels frustrated by Ruby's copycat behavior, and when Ruby gives up the charade and plucks off the fake fingernails. What do their expressions show about how they are feeling? Have students ever felt the same way?

Ruby the Copycat—Follow-Up Activities

☀ Use I-Messages.

Invite students to take turns playing the roles of Angela and Ruby. Ask the student playing Angela to use a conflict-resolution technique (such as I-messages) to express her feelings about being copied. Ask the student playing Ruby to express her need to fit in and be accepted (perhaps by asking Angela to play a game with her, offering to walk home with her, or sharing information about her previous community).

☀ Put Out the Welcome Mat.

Invite students to talk about how they have felt when they were new to a community, a school, or a group. (If students have not experienced being new, ask them to imagine how it might feel.) Then give students each an 8½- by 11-inch sheet of construction paper. Ask them to decorate the paper as a welcome mat. In the center of the mat, have each student write or draw one thing that he or she would do to make a new student, neighbor, or group member feel welcome. Display the welcome mats near the entrance to your classroom. Note: This is a great activity to use if you are welcoming a new student or teacher to your class or school.

☀ On-the-Spot Reporting

Help students learn how copying can affect both the person being copied and the person who is copying. Create a microphone by attaching a ball of aluminum foil to the top of a paper towel tube. Let students take turns being Ruby, Angela, and a news reporter. Have the news reporter describe a specific incident in the book and then interview both Ruby and Angela to find out how they felt at this point in the story. (For example, the news reporter might ask about when they first met, when Ruby first came to school with a red bow, or when Ruby said she was wearing a bridesmaid's dress).

Swimmy—Introducing the Story

Swimmy by Leo Lionni (Pantheon, 1963)

Synopsis: Swimmy helps a school of fish work together to scare off a threatening fish so that they can swim freely in the sea.

Learning Points:

☀ Good things can happen when people work together.

☀ Group members are better able to accomplish a task when they cooperate.

Before reading the story, ask children if they can think of any group activities that depend on the efforts of each individual (for example, playing in a band or in a soccer game). Explain that you are going to demonstrate what happens when a group does and does not work well together. Have everyone sit in a circle, and show the group a ball of yarn. Grasp the end of the yarn and hold it tightly. Then roll the ball to a child across the circle from you. That child then grasps the yarn and holds it, rolling the ball to a classmate. This will eventually form a web. Explain to students that the web only stays together if each participant continues to hold his or her part. If anyone lets go, the web will become a tangled mass of yarn.

Exploring the Story

Read *Swimmy* aloud. Explain that while the individual fish were no match for a predator, they were able to frighten a predator away when they worked together. Discuss the following questions in order to examine the group dynamics that helped the fish succeed.

☀ How did the fish come up with the idea?

☀ What did the little fish have to do to accomplish the plan?

☀ What might have happened if any of the fish didn't cooperate?

☀ Who led the group? What did the leader do that helped bring group members together?

Invite students to describe situations in which they have worked with others for the good of the group, such as making a project together in class, distributing milk cartons at lunchtime, or taking part in a dance recital. Ask students to think about what it took to get along and make the group effort work. For example, did they need to listen to others? Did they need to let others share a task even though they felt they could do it well alone?

Did they need to speak kindly to a group member who acted bossy? Invite children to offer their observations of what was necessary in order to work well together. Write their suggestions on chart paper. (See sample chart below.)

How to Work Well Together

1. Share ideas. Talk to each other.
2. Listen to what others have to say.
3. Speak and act kindly.
4. Trust group members to do their jobs well.
5. Do your part of the job.

✴ Swimmy—Follow-Up Activities ✴

☼ Go, Fish!

Divide the class into groups of four or five students. Give each group a handful of goldfish-shaped crackers, glue, and a paper plate. Have group members work together to glue the crackers in the shape of a large fish to illustrate how the fish swam in the story. For an extra challenge, ask the group to complete the task without talking. Be sure to buy extra crackers for snacking!

Teacher-Tested!

Create Character Webs

Use literature to reinforce positive character traits. Help your students make a character web to highlight a main character's positive attributes, such as being kind and responsible. To make the web, students should write the character's name in the center and the attributes extending around it. After they make the web, have students go back to the story and find examples for each attribute listed.

Contributed by Clarinda Cole
Willard Model Elementary School
Norfolk, Virginia

This activity appeared in *Instructor* magazine, July/August 1995.

Write It Out!

Use the prompts on page 52 to get your students thinking and writing about conflict resolution. They can also add illustrations to support their writing. Encourage children to incorporate some of the skills they have acquired from other conflict resolution activities. You may wish to tailor the questions to meet your students' needs. Younger students may want to focus on how the characters are feeling and why they are feeling that way, while older students might identify the problem and suggest ways to resolve it.

Give each student a pencil and a copy of the reproducible. First, read through the prompts together. Encourage students to work independently or in small groups to write their own stories, using the prompts provided. If desired, have children illustrate their stories. Invite volunteers to share their completed stories with the class or with a partner.

Write It Out!—Follow-Up Activities

☀ Make Conflict Maps.

Help students make simple Conflict Maps for the situations described on the reproducible. Conflict Maps organize the important details: who is involved, what is the problem, what are possible solutions, and what are potential consequences or outcomes of those solutions. (See sample at right.)

> Nancy tells Bea that her painting is a big gloppy mess.
> ↓
> Bea feels hurt and angry.
> ↓
> Bea tells Nancy how she feels and why she is hurt.
> ↓
> Nancy apologizes to Bea.
> ↓
> Bea and Nancy get along.

☀ Act Out the Stories.

Have students work with partners. Let each pair choose one situation from the reproducible and act out the problem and its resolution. Invite volunteers to act out their scenes for the class. For an extra challenge, have students create and act out their own conflict scenarios.

☀ Change the Ending.

Read a picture book aloud, but stop reading before the conflict is resolved. Divide the class into groups. Have each group write, draw, or discuss how they would resolve the conflict. Invite groups to share their ideas with the class.

Write It Out!

Choose one of the scenes below. On a separate sheet of paper, write a story about it. Draw a picture to show how the conflict is resolved. Before you write, ask yourself:

☀ What is the problem?

☀ What could the characters do to solve the problem?

1 Bea and Nancy are sitting together at the art table. Bea is painting a picture.

2 Josh and Dana are playing a board game. Josh thinks Dana cheated. Dana tells him she did not.

3 Edmund is tired and wants to rest. Lois wants Edmund to laugh at her jokes.

4 Both Jan and Martin want the last ice cream sandwich.

Working Toward Peace

Embrace Diversity

No two people are alike; we are surrounded by diversity. Diversity brings a kaleidoscope of lifestyles, beliefs, attitudes, and experiences that can mold and enrich our lives—and that can also be the source of conflict. Because we are different, we don't always view things the same way. Different viewpoints can lead to disagreements and distancing oneself from others. When we consistently view differences as negative and threatening, we begin to believe that there is only one way of thinking: our way. With this type of thinking, conflict resolution is not possible.

Use the activities below to strengthen your students' respect for and appreciation of diversity. Expose them to the understanding that people share basic needs and wants that supersede gender, race, age, and other differences. Foster compassion and acceptance, and you will empower your students to make peaceful choices and to embrace a richer life.

I Am Special. I Am Me!

Use the following activity to reinforce the concept of uniqueness. Give each child the same type of medium-sized fruit or vegetable, such as an apple, orange, potato, or banana. Ask children to study their fruit for five minutes, familiarizing themselves with its shape, size, and any characteristics that make it unique. Then ask students to place their fruit in a large box. Empty the contents of the box and let students try to find their piece of fruit.

Point out that just as no two apples, oranges, and so on are exactly alike, no two people are exactly alike either. Talk about ways in which people differ from each other—in body size and shape, color of eyes, skin, and hair, age, gender, religious beliefs, manner of dress, ethnic background and traditions, and so on.

Peaceable Snowpeople

As a class, decide on three courteous behaviors you'd like to work on for the month, such as sharing, saying *please* and *thank you*, and using words to solve conflicts. Cut three large snowpeople from white paper. Hang them on a blue background and label each with one of the courteous behaviors. Throughout the month, ask students to watch for "snowpeople behaviors." When a student observes one, ask that student to describe the behavior. Then let the observer and the observed each put a snowball on the appropriate snowperson. (You can use clumps of cotton balls for the snowballs.) The goal is to cover all three snowpeople by the end of the month.

Contributed by William Kreidler
Cambridge, Massachusetts

This activity appeared in William Kreidler's column "Caring Classroom," *Instructor* magazine, November/December 1996.

✦ Lend a Hand ✦

Discuss the idea that although people differ from one another, every person has something valuable to offer. For example, a child who likes to act might read a dramatic story to the class. A child who is tall may help get items off a high shelf for someone who can't reach.

Distribute paper and pencils. Ask students to trace one of their hands on a sheet of paper. On each finger, students can write one quality or skill they possess that can help others in some way. Invite volunteers to share their

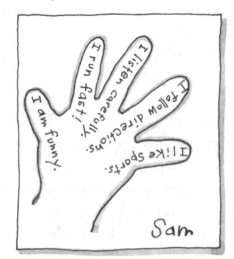

hands with the class, describing one or two qualities and how those qualities can help others. For example, a student who is funny might describe how he entertains his little brother on trips in the car.

See the Similarities

Ask students to list things they think people really need in order to live. Go over the list and help students eliminate things that people want rather than need, such as television and toys. Whittle the list down to the most basic of all needs: food, water, shelter, clothing, and love. Help students understand that all people—regardless of their age, gender, race, ethnic or religious background, skills or abilities—share these same needs. Despite our differences, all people share these important similarities.

We Are the World

Divide the class into groups of three of four children. Give each group a bunch of old magazines and a few pairs of scissors. Ask each group to look through the magazines and cut out ten pictures of people. Explain that the people they find should be diverse in age, gender, ethnic background, physical abilities, skills or talents, interests, and so on. Invite children to glue their pictures onto a large sheet of craft paper to make a class mural. Throughout the week, invite children to bring in from home pictures from old magazines and add them to the mural until it is full. Use the mural as a springboard for discussion (for example, note the differences and similarities between people) and creative writing (write a story about one or more of the people).

Respect—and Celebrate!—Diversity

Help students realize that people differ from one another in many ways: in gender, age, appearance, race, family background, skills, interests, and so on. Here are three ways to celebrate differences:

1. Hold a cultural appreciation week during which students can bring in and talk about toys, songs, or foods that are part of their ethnic or family background.

2. Show students picture books about a variety of ethnic groups and socioeconomic backgrounds. Discuss as a group what they learned.

3. Share stories from newspapers, magazines, or books that demonstrate the wide variety

of skills and interests that people of all ages and both genders have in common. (See Additional Resources, page 64.)

✳ **Let's Play Together!** ✳

Encourage cooperative play with the following activities:

☀ Hold a Block Derby.

In advance, gather small plastic building blocks as well as wheels, axles, and other accessories. You will also need approximately seven paper or plastic bags. In each bag, place a variety of building blocks, including wheels and axles. There should be enough pieces in each bag to build one vehicle. Try to include a similar number and variety of pieces in each bag.

Divide the class into groups of three to four students, and give each group one bag. Explain that they will have 15 minutes to work together to build a vehicle that works (it rolls when pushed or placed on an incline). The groups can create the vehicle in any way they wish, as long as they use every block in their bag. Set up an incline to serve as a raceway where groups can test their cars. If a car does not roll, students can make adjustments as needed within the time limit. When students finish, allow each group to roll its car down the plank for classmates to see. Lead a class discussion about the similarities and differences between the cars. Ask groups to assess how well they worked together.

☀ The Great Divide

Divide the class into groups of three to four students. (Have children wash their hands or use a hand-sanitizing lotion before this and other food-related activities.) Give each group a handful of small treats, such as chocolate kisses, goldfish crackers, or animal crackers. Challenge each group to work together to divide the treats equally among the group members—and then enjoy!

☀ Song Search

Choose three or four popular children's songs, such as "Old MacDonald Had a Farm" and "The Wheels on the Bus." Choose an easily recognizable verse from each song. On

index cards, copy the lyrics of the verses so that there is approximately one line on each card. There should be enough cards so that each student will have one. Shuffle the cards and give one to each student. Have students walk around the class, quietly singing their line and listening for classmates singing the same song. Students with the same song should gather together until everyone has found his or her group. Ask students to arrange their lines in order and sing the verse or the whole song for the class. (Each student can sing his or her line, or the whole group can sing the song or verse together.)

☀ Create a Character.

In advance, gather various art supplies with which children can create a character. For each group of three to four students, fill a paper bag with paper cups, craft sticks, yarn, felt, movable eyes, pipe cleaners, and glue. Be sure to include the same number and variety of supplies in each bag.

Divide the class into small groups, and give each group a bag. Explain that groups will use the supplies to create their own unique character (it can be a person, an animal, or an imaginary creature). They will need to agree on what kind of creature it will be and what they will name it. Display their characters and discuss how they are similar and different. (They are made of the same materials, but each is unique and special).

NOTE: After students work together in cooperative activities, take time to talk about what it was like to work together. Invite students to tell whether they encountered any problems while working together and how they resolved them.

Make a Peace Table

Set up a table in your classroom where students can meet to solve problems. You might put a desk and two chairs in a corner of the room and cover the desk with a cheerful tablecloth. Post reminders nearby to help students remember the tools for conflict resolution: using I-messages, listening carefully, speaking with respect, and trying to find a solution that satisfies everyone involved. You may wish to establish guidelines for working at the peace table—speaking in quiet voices, using peaceful language, and so on.

Contributed by Lourdes Ballesteros
North Miami, Florida

This activity appeared in *Instructor* magazine, July/August 1994.

Catch the Spirit of Kindness!

Encourage kids to catch the spirit of kindness by making their own Kindness Catcher! Give each student scissors, crayons, and a copy of the reproducibles on pages 59–60. Invite students to color the pictures before they cut them out. Demonstrate how to assemble the catchers by following the directions on page 59. Kindness Catchers are fun to use—and they provide helpful reminders of conflict resolution strategies.

Brighten-Their-Day Calendar

Use the reproducible calendar on page 61 for every month of the school year! In each square, you'll find a helpful reminder about how class members can brighten each day. Simply fill in the name of the month and refer to a calendar to fill in the numbers accurately. (To reinforce calendar skills, give students each a copy of the reproducible and have them fill in the missing information.) Invite students to color in a box or draw an illustration each time they do one of the tasks.

Head for Camp Kindness

Encourage kindness in your classroom with this fun, reproducible game that children can play on their own. Reproduce the game board on pages 62–63, and invite students to color it. Then tape the pages together. (For greater durability, laminate the game board and tape it in a file folder.) Before beginning, gather students around to demonstrate how the game is played. To play, players take turns moving their pieces forward the number they rolled on the die and following the directions in the space they land on. (Kids can use chips, beans, or other small objects for playing pieces.) The game ends when every player reaches FINISH.

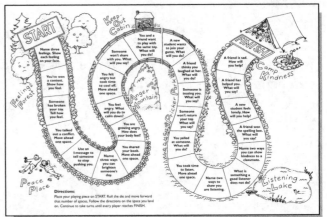

Catch the Spirit of Kindness!

To Assemble:

1. Cut along the dotted lines. Fold as shown to make your own Kindness Catcher.

2. Put each thumb and index finger into one of the pockets underneath the Kindness Catcher.

3. Stretch out your thumbs and fingers, bring them together, and pull them apart in the other direction to open and close the catcher.

To Play:

1. Ask a friend to pick a picture on the top of the Kindness Catcher. Open and close the catcher the same number of times as the number of smiling faces you see.

2. Look inside the catcher. Ask the friend to choose one of the kind acts. Look at the number on that picture. Open and close the Kindness Catcher that many times.

3. Ask the friend to choose one of the flaps and look under it. Read the kind wish inside. Urge your friend to help it come true!

° WITH THE PRINTED SIDE FACEDOWN, FOLD IN HALF ALONG DIAGONAL.

FOLD AGAIN

° NOW OPEN AND LAY FLAT AGAIN, THEN FOLD IN HALF ALONG OTHER DIAGONAL.

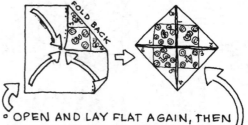

° OPEN AND LAY FLAT AGAIN, THEN FOLD BACK EACH CORNER TO TOUCH AT THE CENTER.

° NOW, TURN THIS SQUARE OVER, AND FOLD BACK THESE CORNERS TO TOUCH AT THE CENTER.

° FOLD THIS SQUARE IN HALF, OPEN IT, THEN FOLD IN HALF THE OTHER WAY.

OPEN

FOLD AGAIN, THEN OPEN.

° NOW PEEL BACK "SMILEY" CORNERS, AND INSERT INDEX FINGERS AND THUMBS.

Catch the Spirit of Kindness!

Brighten Their Day!

(month)

Sunday	Monday	Tuesday	Wednesday	Thursday	Friday	Saturday
Sing someone a song.	Write someone a letter.	Say five kind words.	Sit beside someone new.	Smile at every-one you see.	Wish someone a nice day.	Offer to help carry something.
Pay someone a compliment.	Give someone a hug.	Invite a friend over.	Make a bead bracelet for someone.	Make a greeting card for someone.	Read to a younger child.	Draw a picture for someone.
Put on a puppet show.	Share a snack.	Take time to listen.	Laugh at someone's joke.	Give someone a flower or a greeting card.	Paint a picture for someone.	Send someone a postcard.
Share.	Laugh with others.	Push a friend on a swing.	Set the table.	Greet others with a smile.	Share happy thoughts.	Make a gift for someone.
Call an older relative on the phone.	Write a kind letter to someone.	Hold the door open for someone else.	Help someone with a chore.	Say *please* and *thank you.*	Share a toy.	Write a poem for someone.

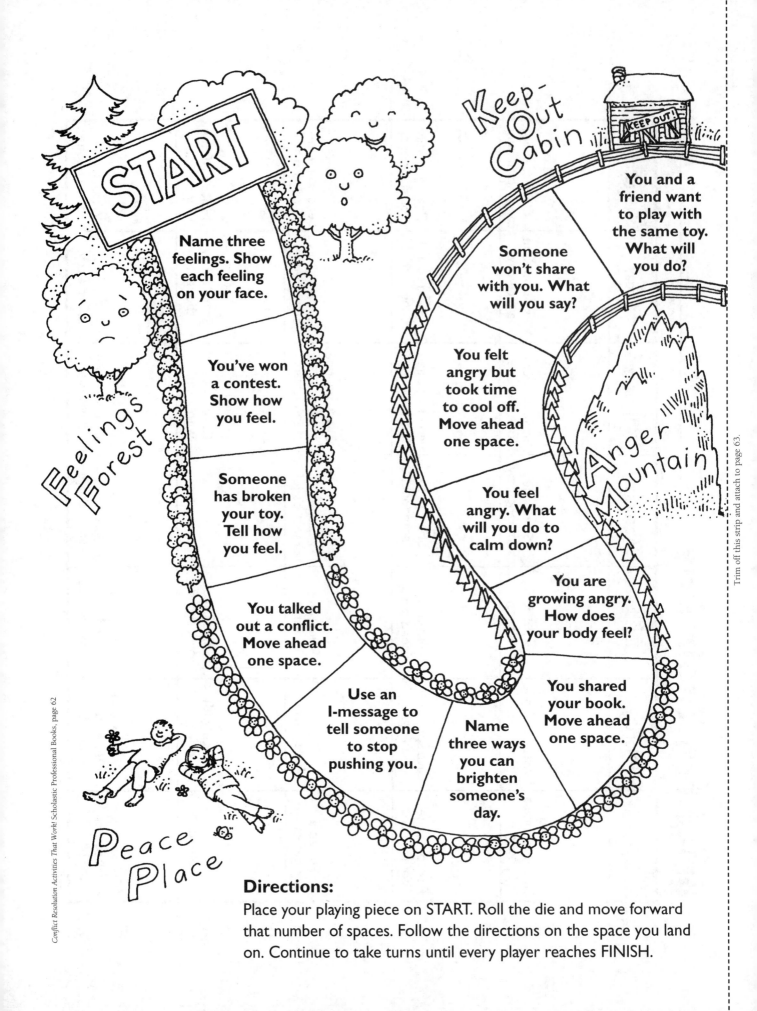

START

Name three feelings. Show each feeling on your face.

You've won a contest. Show how you feel.

Someone has broken your toy. Tell how you feel.

You talked out a conflict. Move ahead one space.

Use an I-message to tell someone to stop pushing you.

Name three ways you can brighten someone's day.

You shared your book. Move ahead one space.

You are growing angry. How does your body feel?

You feel angry. What will you do to calm down?

You felt angry but took time to cool off. Move ahead one space.

Someone won't share with you. What will you say?

You and a friend want to play with the same toy. What will you do?

Keep-Out Cabin

KEEP OUT!

Anger Mountain

Feelings Forest

Peace Place

Directions:

Place your playing piece on START. Roll the die and move forward that number of spaces. Follow the directions on the space you land on. Continue to take turns until every player reaches FINISH.

Trim off this strip and attach to page 63.

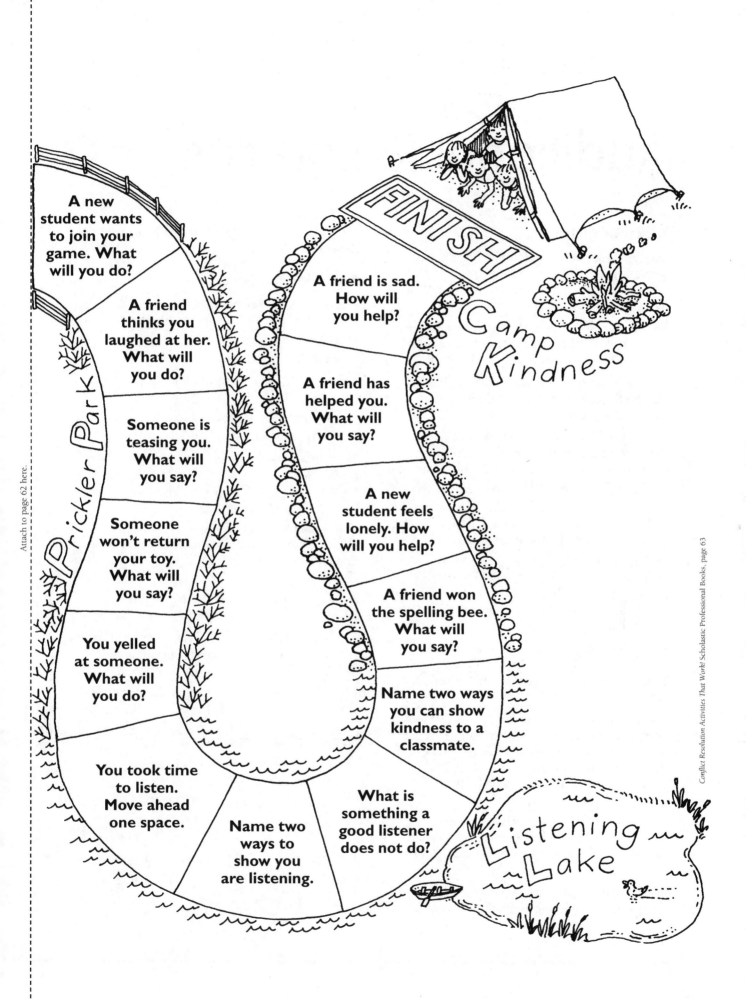

A new student wants to join your game. What will you do?

A friend thinks you laughed at her. What will you do?

Someone is teasing you. What will you say?

Someone won't return your toy. What will you say?

You yelled at someone. What will you do?

You took time to listen. Move ahead one space.

You took time to listen. Move ahead one space.

Name two ways to show you are listening.

What is something a good listener does not do?

Name two ways you can show kindness to a classmate.

A friend won the spelling bee. What will you say?

A new student feels lonely. How will you help?

A friend has helped you. What will you say?

A friend is sad. How will you help?

FINISH

Camp Kindness

Pricker Park

Listening Lake

Conflict Resolution Activities That Work! Scholastic Professional Books, page 63

Additional Resources

Books for Children

Amazing Grace by Mary Hoffman (Dial Books for Young Readers, 1991). Grace loves to act. When Grace is told she cannot play the role of Peter Pan, she proves her classmates wrong.

Best Enemies by Kathleen Leverich (Greenwillow Books, 1989). Priscilla makes a new friend—who turns out to be the best enemy she's ever had.

Clarissa by Carol Talley (Marsh Media, 1992). Clarissa the cow wishes she could be special—and one day discovers she is.

A Friend for Growl Bear by Margot Austin (HarperCollins, 1999). Animals won't befriend a young bear until they learn more about him—and discover a lonely bear who needs a friend.

The Hating Book by Charlotte Zolotow (Harper & Row, 1969). Miscommunication foils a friendship until the two friends talk things out.

It's Mine! by Leo Lionni (Knopf, 1986). Three selfish frogs spend their days fighting over air, water, and land until a heavy storm brings them together in fear—and shows them how important it is to share and work together.

Katharine's Doll by Elizabeth Winthrop (E.P. Dutton, 1983). Katherine and Molly are best friends until Katherine gets a new doll and they begin competing over her.

Matthew and Tilly by Rebecca C. Jones (Dutton Children's Books, 1991). Matthew and Tilly are best friends, but even best friends sometimes argue. When an argument sends them separate ways, Matthew and Tilly miss each other and decide to make up.

Mean Soup by Betsy Everitt (Harcourt Brace Jovanovich, 1992). When Horace has a terrible day, his mother helps him release his anger in an unexpected way.

Smoky Night by Eve Bunting (Harcourt Brace & Company, 1994). In the midst of a riot, a young girl and her mother reach out to others they used to avoid.

Books for Teachers

Creative Conflict Resolution by William J. Kreidler (Scott Foresman and Company, 1984).

Dealing With Anger by Marianne Johnston (PowerKids Press, 1996).

Dealing With Arguments by Lisa K. Adams (PowerKids Press, 1997).

Dealing With Someone Who Won't Listen by Lisa K. Adams (PowerKids Press, 1997).

The Friendly Classroom for a Small Planet: A Handbook on Creative Approaches to Living and Problem Solving for Children by Priscilla Prutzman (New Society Publishers, 1988).

How to Talk So Kids Can Learn at Home and in School by Adele Faber and Elaine Mazlish, with teachers Lisa Nyberg and Rosalyn Anstine Templeton (Simon and Schuster, 1995).

Teaching Conflict Resolution Through Children's Literature by William J. Kreidler (Scholastic, 1994).

Teaching Young Children in Violent Times: Building a Peaceable Classroom by Diane E. Levin, Ph.D. (Educators for Social Responsibility, 1994).

Waging Peace in Our Schools by Linda Lantieri and Janet Patti (Beacon Press, 1996).

Music Builds Harmony!

These catchy tunes help build community as children sing them together.

16 Songs Kids Love to Sing performed by Pat and Tex LaMountain (Northeast Foundation for Children).

Teaching Peace by Red Grammer, (Red Note).

Down the Do-Re-Mi by Red Grammer, (Red Note).